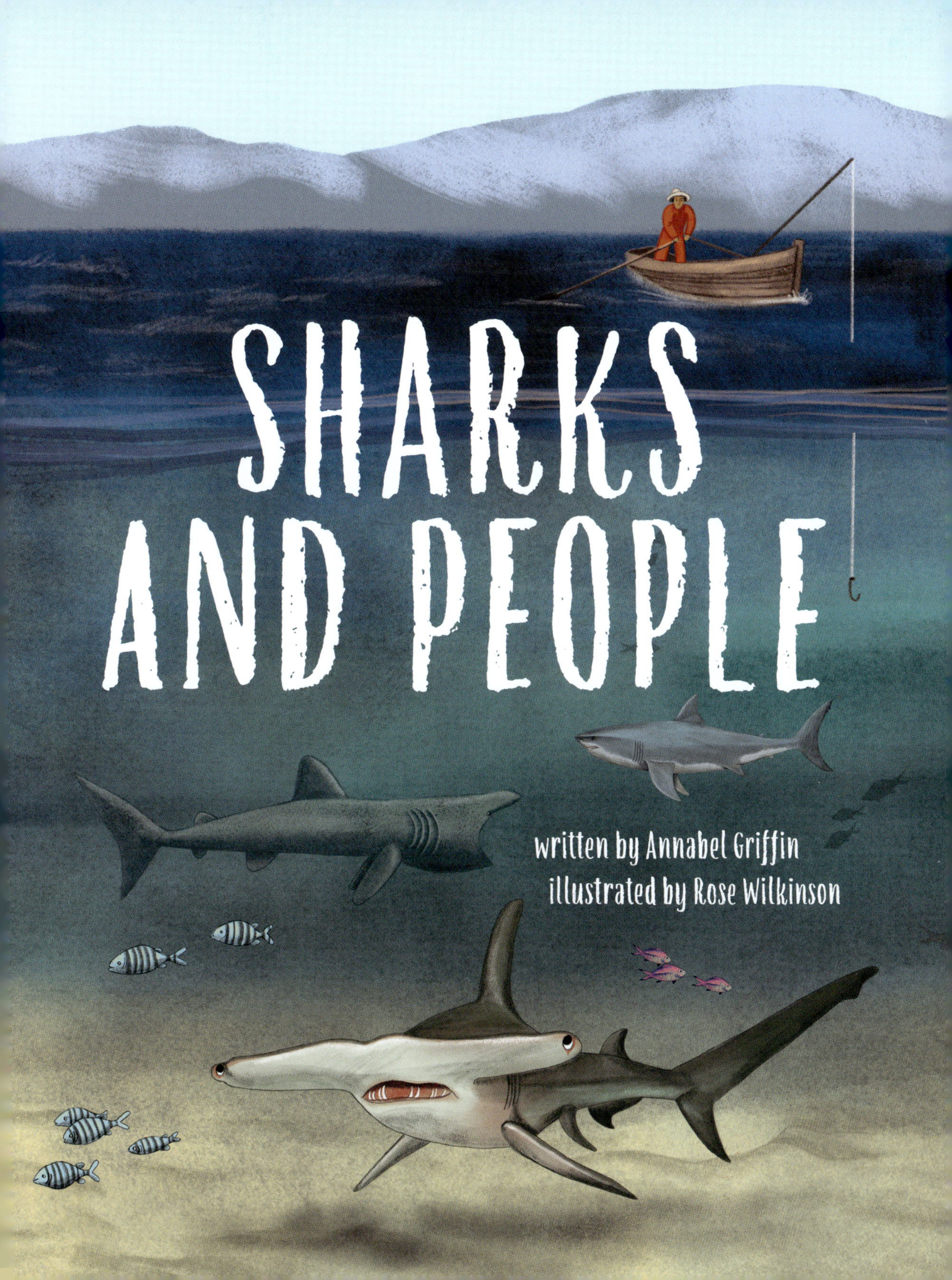
SHARKS
AND PEOPLE
written by Annabel Griffin
illustrated by Rose Wilkinson

First published in 2022 by Hungry Tomato Ltd
F15, Old Bakery Studios, Blewetts Wharf, Malpas Road, Truro, Cornwall, TR1 1QH, UK.

A CIP catalog record for this book is available from the British Library.

ISBN 978-1-915461-11-7

Manufactured in the USA

Discover more at
www.hungrytomato.com

CONTENTS

Words in **bold** can be found in the glossary.

SHARK AND PEOPLE

Lots of people are afraid of sharks, but they have much more reason to be scared of us!

Shark vs. human

Shark attacks are very rare and most sharks are harmless to humans. On the other hand, we kill millions of sharks every year!

Sharks are awesome!

There are many reasons why sharks deserve respect. Among other things, they help keep our oceans healthy and may even help fight **climate change!**

Save the sharks

More and more sharks are becoming **endangered** all the time. What can we do to save them?

SCARED OF SHARKS?

Sharks have a reputation for being big, scary man-eaters. In reality, most sharks are completely harmless to humans.

Look out for signs

On some beaches where shark sightings are common, signs are posted to tell you if it's safe to enter the water.

What are the chances?

Shark attacks are extremely rare. You have a much higher chance of being killed by a firework than by a shark, and that's very, very unlikely!

Surfers not seals

Surfers are the most likely to be attacked because sharks might mistake a surfboard for a seal. This is still incredibly rare.

Mistaken identity

Sharks don't really want to eat people. It is thought that most shark attacks happen because the shark has mistaken the person for something else. They will often take one bite and then let go.

WHY SHARKS MATTER

We often focus on sharks as ferocious killers, but many other sea creatures rely on them for survival.

Keeping the balance

Sharks help keep the numbers of other sea creatures under control. For example

shortfin mako sharks eat bluefin tuna

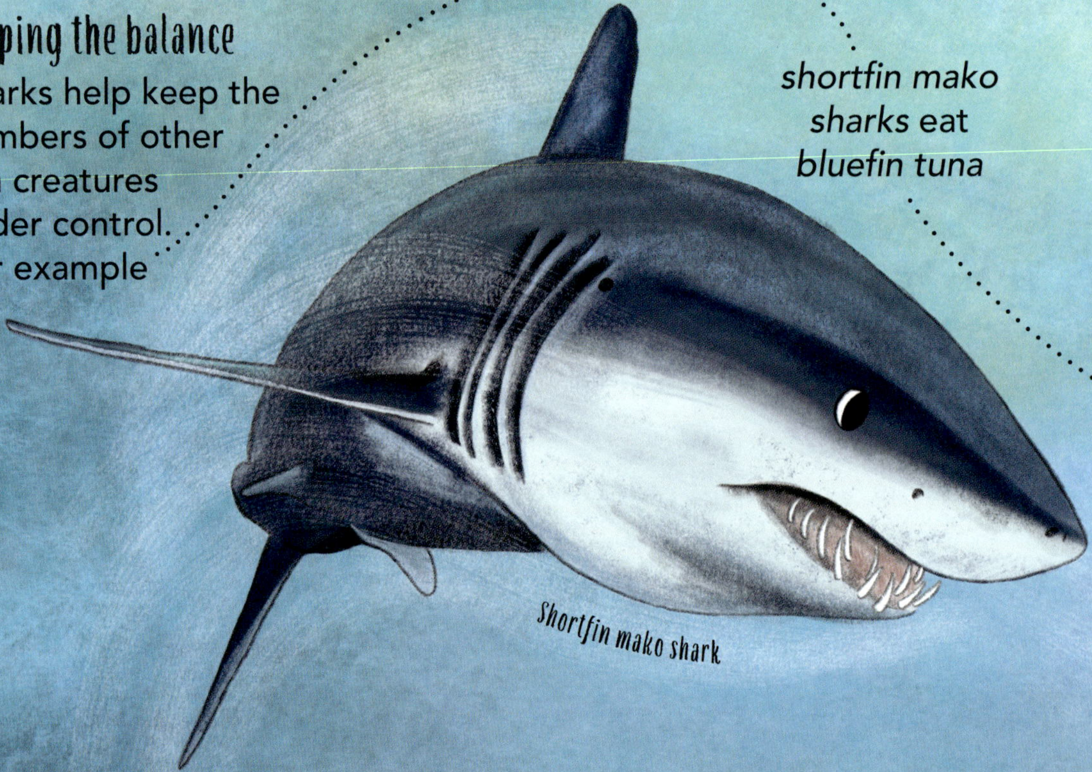

Reef protectors

Sharks protect coral reefs by eating larger fish that live around them. Too many large fish would mean that lots of smaller ones would get eaten. Without small fish to eat **algae,** reefs can become smothered in it, making them unhealthy.

Sucking up

Some fish, like *remoras (suckerfish),* rely on sharks for food. They feed on **parasites** and dead skin found on sharks' bodies.

then *mackerel* numbers could fall, as more of them become tuna food.

if shark numbers fell, the number of tuna could rise

THREATS TO SHARKS

Sadly, many different types of shark are now in danger of becoming **extinct.** Here are some of the reasons why.

Overfishing

Overfishing is the biggest threat to sharks. Millions of sharks are killed by humans every year. Parts of their bodies are sold for food and to make other products.

Climate change

Important **habitats** where some sharks live, such as coral reefs, are being destroyed by climate change.

Ocean pollution

Huge amounts of our waste ends up in the ocean, causing **pollution.** This can damage habitats and release harmful chemicals into the water.

Sharks and other sea creatures can swallow plastic waste, making them ill.

ENDANGERED SHARKS

Many sharks are now critically endangered. This means there is a high risk of them becoming extinct if nothing is done to save them. Here are some of the most endangered species.

Missing Shark?

The last offical sighting of a Pondicherry shark was in 1979. They may already be extinct.

Rare angels

Angel sharks live on sandy seabeds. Many types of angel shark are now critically endangered.

Famous but fragile

Hammerhead sharks are probably one of the best known shark families, but some of its members are in serious danger.

Big fins, big problems!

Oceanic whitetips are overfished for their large fins, which are used to make *shark fin soup*, a popular dish in parts of Southeast Asia.

Wrong place, wrong time

These rare sharks are in danger from being caught accidentally in fishing nets.

SWIMMING WITH SHARKS

Shark tourism can make many people's dreams of diving with sharks come true. Would you be brave enough?

Helping sharks

Shark tourism can be good for sharks as local people can make their money from tourists rather than fishing for sharks.

Shark watch

Many **tourists** prefer watching sharks from the safety of a boat, but boats that get too close can harm the sharks.

Cage diving

Cage diving can be a good way to see more dangerous sharks up close, as the steel cage protects the divers.

Should you feed sharks?

Some diving tours allow you to feed sharks, but some people believe this could lead to more shark attacks, as sharks might start to think people equal food.

SAVING SHARKS

With so many endangered sharks, what is being done to protect them, and how can we help?

Keeping track

Scientists attach **tracking devices** (or tags) to sharks' fins. This allows them to track their movement and habits, and keep an eye on their numbers.

Stop overfishing

Shark sanctuaries are areas of ocean where shark fishing is forbidden. Many countries have now set up sanctuaries in areas that they control.

Did you know?

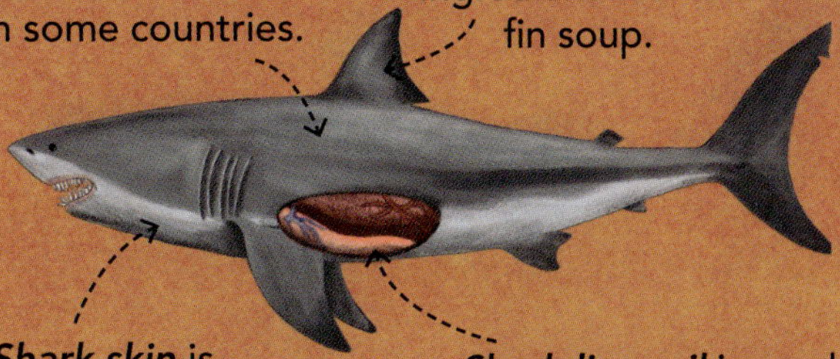

SHOP SMART

Avoid food and other products that contain shark parts.

SHARKS ARE FRIENDS, NOT FOOD!

OCEANS

Many people around the world are working hard to clean up plastics and pollution in our oceans. You can help by **recycling** and not buying plastic products.

IMPORTANT FACTS

Moving out

Climate change is heating up our oceans. As cold areas become inviting, and other parts become too warm, some sharks are moving into new waters. This could be bad news for other sea creatures already living there!

Climate change will affect reef sharks habitats.

Who's in more danger?

Every year, up to 100 million sharks are killed by humans, while on average, fewer than 5 people will die because of a shark attack.

Where do most shark attacks happen?

Florida is sometimes called the shark bite capital of the world, as it usually has the highest number of shark attacks each year.

A seaside shark net

No more nets!

Some beaches are surrounded by large nets in the water to stop sharks swimming too close to people. Unfortunately, sharks and other sea creatures can easily get trapped in them.

TRUE OR FALSE?

Can you guess which of these facts about sharks are true or false?

Shark fins can treat illnesses

Some people believe eating shark fins is good for you, but this is ***FALSE.*** Shark fins are actually very high in mercury, a metal which can be dangerous to humans.

Shark fin soup

Sharks live in rivers

While most sharks only live in oceans, it's ***TRUE*** that a few types of shark can be found in rivers. Bull sharks can live in both seas and rivers.

Bull shark

Sharks don't have predators

This is ***FALSE.*** Killer whales occasionally attack sharks, and some sharks will prey on their own kind.

Killer whale

However, the biggest predator of sharks is humans.

A shark fishing boat

Bigger sharks are more dangerous

This is ***FALSE***. In fact, the two largest sharks, the basking shark and the whale shark are very gentle and only eat tiny sea creatures, like plankton.

Whale shark

GLOSSARY

algae
Plant-like living things that usually live in or near water.

climate change
Rising temperatures on the Earth, which are affecting weather around the world. Ocean temperatures are rising too, which is causing problems for some plants and animals that live in them, including sharks.

endangered
At a high risk of becoming extinct (see below).

extinct
When a type of plant or animal no longer exists anywhere on Earth.

habitats
The place where an animal or plant lives.

overfishing
When too many fish are being caught.

parasites
Living things that live on or inside another living thing to survive.

pollution
When air, water or land on Earth becomes unhealthy because of trash, chemicals, or other harmful things within it.

recycling
Turning something that would otherwise be thrown away into something that can be used again.

shark sanctuaries
An area of ocean where shark fishing has been made illegal.

shark tourism
When people pay to go and watch or dive with sharks.

tourists
People who are on vacation.

tracking devices
Machines that attach to something so that its location can be tracked.

INDEX

About the Author

Annabel is a writer and artist based in Cornwall, UK, who writes children's books with a focus on animals and the natural world. She is the author of the *One Planet* series, about Earth and the environment, and *What Can I See in the Wild?*, published by Beetle Books. In her free time, Annabel enjoys drawing, hiking, and gardening. She is never without a good book.

About the Illustrator

Rose is an illustrator, artist and educator from Hereford, UK, now living and working in London. Her mediums of choice are watercolor, gouache, pencil and Procreate.

Picture Credits

(abbreviations: t = top; b = bottom; c = center; l = left; r = right)

shutterstock: Wildestanimal 18cr; Igor Kruglikov 18bl; Yann Hubert 19cr; Rose Makin 19bl; Photomaniakung 20cr; Stefan Pircher 20br; Tory Kallman 21tl; Hannah van herk 21cr; Krzysztof odziomek 21br.

Every effort has been made to trace the copyright holders, and we apologize in advance for any unintentional omissions. We would be pleased to insert the appropriate acknowledgments in any subsequent edition of this publication.